It's Real

The Battle of Gods

and your actions to guarantee victory

Oluseyi Simeon

Harmony Publishing

For permission requests, write to the publisher at the addresses below:

Harmony Publishing
Plot 8, Providence Street, Opposite Halifield School,
Lekki Phase 1, Lagos, Nigeria.
+2347032212481
publish@harmonypublishing.com.ng

First Edition: November, 2024

ISBN: 978-978-60692-9-6

Printed in Nigeria

DEDICATION

To my wife, Stella, for the strength and support you provided all through the period of our battles.

To my children, Oluwanifemi, Olamilekan and Ifejolalo, the emotional stress you endured, your faith in me and your silent prayers also kept me.

To my mother-in-law, Elizabeth, who has ever been our backbone by her prayers and support right from day one and throughout the dark period.

ACKNOWLEDGEMENTS

To my wife, Stella Simeon. You have been a co-traveller in my journey of life, and we have faced all battles together. I appreciate your courage even though, sometimes, you broke down and we did cry together.

I also salute my wonderful children, Oluwanifemi, Olamilekan and Ifejolalo, who also learnt, during those dark years, some deep lessons of life. You all endured and believed in God with us.

And to my mother-in-law, Elizabeth Ebhonum. You are a real mother. God used you as a solid rock behind us. You believed in us and watched over us like a hawk.

My profound gratitude also goes to Pastor Sunday Odunuga and Pastor (Mummy) Bimpe Odunuga of the Redeemed Christian Church of God, Kingdom Palace. Your impact in our lives also helped us to sail through.

How can I forget Reverend C.C. Orgu, the Provost of LIFE Theological Seminary, Foursquare Gospel Church in Nigeria! You are one of those whom God used to lay a solid foundation for my Christian faith and knowledge.

I also want to sincerely acknowledge Dr D.K. Olukoya, the General Overseer of the Mountain of Fire and Miracles Ministries. Even though I have not met you physically, you have been a powerful instrument of deliverance in my life and for my entire family. God made me to know you at the right time during my period of battles; otherwise, I would have been wasted. God used your teachings, prayers and counselling to rescue me and my family.

No one outgrows spiritual warfare

– Dr DK Olukoya

TABLE OF CONTENTS

CHAPTER 1

David & Goliath

"In the battle of life, you must fight, either you like it or not.

You must fight to take back what belongs to you.

You must fight to defend your destiny."

–Dr DK Olukoya

> *...And the Philistine said unto David, Am I a dog that thou comest to me with staves? And the Philistine cursed David by his gods. And the Philistine said to David, Come to me, and I will give thy flesh unto the fowls of the air, and to the beasts of the field. Then said David to the Philistine, Thou comest to me with a sword, and with a spear, and with a shield: but I come to thee in the name of the Lord* of hosts, the God of the armies of Israel, whom thou hast defied. (I Sam 17:43-45)

Life is characterised by different difficulties and struggles, many of which are not ordinary but conflicts between unseen forces. They are spiritual in various dimensions.

We need to understand and appreciate this fact to successfully navigate through life. Many could not attain their potentials because incomprehensible situations hindered them at one point of their endeavour. While we may think these issues are just circumstantial, most times, they are not. Life situations are mostly spiritual.

The story of David and Goliath is a rich example of life's constant battles. Whether we believe it or not is irrelevant. The forces of light and darkness are always at war in the spirit realm.

> *...And he stood and cried unto the armies of Israel, and said unto them, Why are ye come out to set your battle in array? am not I a Philistine, and ye servants to Saul? choose you a man for you, and let him come down to me. (I Sam 17:8).*

Goliath challenged the children of Israel on the battlefront and defiled the God of Israel. King Saul and the army of Israel could not confront him until David, a little boy, arrived on the scene. David was enraged by how Goliath boasted and how he defiled the God of Israel. David knew God's power and might to deliver from any situation of life. He had a testimony in the scriptures.

> *But the people that do know their God shall be strong, and do exploits (Daniel 11:32)*

David volunteered and matched forward against Goliath, albeit with his own choice of weaponry, not the conventional one used on the battlefield but one proven and used by God through him. Goliath was surprised to see David, a small rat, coming to challenge him. More interestingly, David came with only one staff.

> *..And when the Philistine looked about, and saw David, he disdained him: for he was but a youth, and ruddy, and of a fair countenance. And the Philistine said unto David, Am I a dog, which thou comest to me with staves? And the Philistine cursed David by his gods. (I Sam 17:42.)*

Meanwhile, Goliath reckoned that for David to challenge him, he could not have been an ordinary boy. In order not to leave anything to chances, despite his might, Goliath had to invoke his gods against David. **He cursed David by his gods.**

This clearly shows that many of the situations we face and consider to be ordinary may not be after all. Those we deal with each day may be invoking the power of their gods against us. We must know that many people are occults. Life is a battlefield, and people do not take things lightly.

My Experience of Office Battle

After many office politics and gang-ups, I lost my job. I was diligent, hard-working and always meeting my deliverables. However, where there are conspiracies, you can never survive despite any good deeds you do. I was thrown into the job market.

Life was tough as I had a family to cater for. Nevertheless, I pulled through by God's grace. Because of my good qualifications and experience, I was privileged to get short-listed for roles several times. But the unfortunate side of the story was that I never landed any of the roles. Then there was this role I was eventually called for after many disappointments.

I also remembered I had opportunities to speak with some job consultants and hiring managers. Some of them confessed that although I was the best amongst other candidates, the clients simply preferred someone else. At that point, I knew something must be amiss. So, for this last opportunity, I fasted and prayed seriously all through the selection process. I secured the job at last.

When I resumed, the driver to the person I took over from confessed to me that the former jobholder went after powers to retain his position when he realized that he would be sacked. As his driver, he drove him to those places. Though the selection for the role was done confidentially, because the job holder had not been sacked at that time, he knew what was going on, somehow, and did all he could to scuttle the process.

When I resumed at the role, I also discovered that one of the junior colleagues, who was expecting to take over the position of the former jobholder, also went about seeking powers to ensure no new person was considered for the position. This confirms the scriptures:

> *For we wrestle not against flesh and blood, but against principalities, against powers, against the rulers of the darkness of this world, against spiritual wickedness in high places. Eph. 6:12*

People will go to any extent to get whatever they want or secure whatever belongs to them. We must always remember that life is a battlefield.

David, did not take Goliath's outburst for granted and responded immediately and appropriately. As for David, he came against Goliath in the name of the God of Israel. ***So, it's the battle of Gods.***

> *Then said David to the Philistine, Thou comest to me with a sword, and with a spear, and with a shield: but I come to thee in the name of the Lord* of hosts, the God of the armies of Israel, whom thou hast defied. I Sam 17: 45.

A man will be wasted if he is complacent in the battle of life. People are more demonic and hyper-spiritual than we can ever imagine. They may look innocent and naïve; however, they are serious and take things seriously. They may look friendly and gentle, but they can be potential enemies. They understand we are all on a battlefield, competing. Only a fool will take things for granted.

The fact that David had experienced the delivering power of God before his encounter with Goliath made it easy for him to trust God. He knew his God:

> *And David said unto Saul, Thy servant kept his father's sheep, and there came a lion, and a bear, and took a lamb out of the flock. And I went out after him, and smote him, and delivered it out of his mouth: and when he arose against me, I caught him by his beard, and smote him, and slew him. Thy servant slew both the lion and the bear: and this uncircumcised Philistine shall be as one of them, seeing he hath defied the armies of the living God. David said moreover, The Lord* that delivered me out of the paw of the lion, and out of the paw of the bear, he will deliver me out of the hand of this Philistine. And Saul said unto David, Go, and the *Lord* be with thee. (I Sam 17:34-37)

God wants us to trust him in fighting our battles. He does not want us to be complacent or naïve on the battlefield of life. The kingdom of darkness with its agents means business and only wants to kill and destroy:

> *The thief comes only to steal and kill and destroy; I have come that they may have life, and have it to the full. (John 10:10)*

By rejecting King Saul's offer, David refused to trust in the arm of flesh. For one, he had not proven Saul's weaponry. Meanwhile, if it did not work for King Saul and his army against the Philistines, it couldn't have worked for him. David chose to rely on his kind of weapon through which God had once delivered him.

> *And Saul armed David with his armour, and he put an helmet of brass upon his head; also he armed him with a coat of mail. And David girded his sword upon his armour, and he assayed to go; for he had not proved it. And David said unto Saul, I cannot go with these; for I have not proved them. And David put them off him. (I Sam 17: 38-39)*

We must understand God and trust Him absolutely. Sometimes, people will want to offer you help not because they like you but because they don't want you to succeed. They are failures, so they would never want you to surpass them. We need to be very careful and discerning. Not all helps are helps in the real sense. Some helps entrap you or inhibit your success.

There are stories of friends who introduced others to the occult even though they were fellow Christians. Although many are professed Christians, secretly, they visit other places to seek powers and spiritual helps. So, when you see them in church praying and singing, if you are not discerning enough, you may be in danger when you follow them or take their advice.

Your Involvement in this Battle

- You must be born again. This is not negotiable.
- You must live a holy life.
- You must know your God. Having a good relationship with God makes this possible.

- You must know your enemies and their gods. Despite the size and might of Goliath, David knew that Goliath and his gods were no match for the God of Israel.

- You must be ready to fight. David faced Goliath with the help of his God. While King Saul and the army of Israel were afraid to face Goliath, David confronted him. Goliath was surprised at David's audacious move. Prayer is a potent weapon to use in this fight. Hence, your prayer altar must be on fire.

- Never rely on the unproven weaponry of your friends or people who pretend to assist you.

- Never spare the enemies. David cut Goliath's head. In the battlefield of life, the winner takes it all. If you spare the enemies, you may be setting yourself up for future battles.

CHAPTER 2

Samson & Delilah

"Never share your secrets with anybody.

It will destroy you."

- Chanakya

> *And it came to pass afterward, that he loved a woman in the valley of Sorek, whose name was Delilah. And the lords of the Philistines came up unto her, and said unto her, Entice him, and see wherein his great strength lieth, and by what means we may prevail against him, that we may bind him to afflict him; and we will give thee every one of us eleven hundred pieces of silver. And Delilah said to Samson, Tell me, I pray thee, wherein thy great strength lieth, and wherewith thou mightest be bound to afflict thee. (Judges 16:4-6)*

The Philistines were tormenting the people of Israel at a time in their history. They cried to God and He provided a saviour in Samson to deliver them from the Philistines:

> *And the children of Israel did evil again in the sight of the LORD; and the LORD delivered them into the hand of the Philistines forty years. And there was a certain man of Zorah, of the family of the Danites, whose name was Manoah; and his wife was barren, and bare not. And the angel of the LORD appeared unto the woman, and said unto her, Behold now, thou art barren, and bearest not: but thou shalt conceive, and bear a son. Now therefore beware, I pray thee, and drink not wine nor strong drink, and eat not any unclean thing. For, lo, thou shalt conceive, and bear a son; and no razor shall come on his head: for the child shall be a Nazarite unto God from the womb: and he shall begin to deliver Israel out of the hand of the Philistines. (Judges 13:1-5)*

Samson was a man with extraordinary strength. He was a Nazarite unto God from birth. We can rightly say Samson was God-personified to deliver Israel. Unfortunately, Samson's weakness was women.

> *And Samson went down to Timnath, and saw a woman in Timnath of the daughters of the Philistines. And he came up, and told his father and his mother, and said, I have seen a woman in Timnath of the daughters of the Philistines: now therefore get her for me to wife. (Judges 14:1-2)*

He wasn't just into ordinary women but women from the enemy's camp.

> *Then his father and his mother said unto him, Is there never a woman among the daughters of thy brethren, or among all my people, that thou goest to take a wife of the uncircumcised Philistines? And Samson said unto his father, Get her for me; for she pleaseth me well." (Judges 14:3)*

> *Then went Samson to Gaza, and saw there an harlot, and went in unto her. And it was told the Gazites, saying, Samson is come hither. And they compassed him in, and laid wait for him all night in the gate of the city, and were quiet all the night, saying, In the morning, when it is day, we shall kill him. (Judges 16:1-2)*

My Friend called Kelvin

Back in the day, I was working for one of the top-tier banks in the country as an inspector. As inspectors, we travelled to several states auditing the bank branches, apparently spending most of the time away from home, families and wives.

Kelvin was a colleague of mine then—very brilliant and smart guy. He was also diligent and dutiful. He was a Christian too. Unfortunately, he fell into the sin of adultery. I guess he must have listened to advice from some of our colleagues who engaged in the act. The fact that we were often away from home and almost living in hotels also did not help him. I feel he was not just disciplined enough to depend on God's strength. What is more, he followed evil counsel from so-called friends.

We see a similar pattern in the story of Samson. The sad aspect for Samson was that he never realized ***he was fighting with the gods of the Philistines.*** He had used his strength so many times and prevailed. So, he felt he could always win the battle against men. However, when the battle is between gods, a man's strength is useless.

> *...He will keep the feet of his saints, And the wicked shall be silent in darkness; For by strength shall no man prevail. (1 Samuel 2:9)*

Samson got entangled with Delilah, one of daughters of the Philistines. This time around, the lords of the Philistines knew the only way to defeat him was to know his source of strength. Without that, no one could match him in any physical contest.

> *And the lords of the Philistines came up unto her, and said unto her, Entice him, and see wherein his great strength lieth, and by what means we may prevail against him, that we may bind him to afflict him; and we will give thee every one of us eleven hundred pieces of silver. And Delilah said to Samson, Tell me, I pray thee, wherein thy great strength lieth, and wherewith thou mightest be bound to afflict thee. (Judges 16:5-6)*

One powerful weapon of the enemy that easily entraps men is sex. If a man cannot exercise self-control when it comes to women and sex, he will fall eventually. The enemy has destroyed men with good careers, marriages, and relationships and great prospects using sex.

> *For by means of a whorish woman a man is brought to a piece of bread: and the adulteress will hunt for the precious life. (Proverbs. 6:26)*

Samson thought he was smart with Delilah and continued with the game. He didn't realize that when it comes to the game of women and sex, the best of men will fall.

> *For she hath cast down many wounded: yea, many strong men have been slain by her (Proverbs 7:26)*

With much pressure from Delilah, Samson yielded and told her the source of his strength.

> *And when Delilah saw that he had told her all his heart, she sent and called for the lords of the Philistines, saying, come up this once, for he hath shewed me all his heart. Then the lords of the Philistines came up unto her, and brought money in their hand. And she made him sleep upon her knees; and she called for a man, and she caused him to shave off the seven locks of his head;*

> *and she began to afflict him, and his strength went from him. (Judges 16:18-19.)*

Samson had the God of Israel in him. He had strength and was powerful, but his inordinate affection, especially for sex and daughters of the enemy, ruined his life. The lords of the Philistines knew that Samson was not ordinary. All along, they had fought Samson with their god, the "Dragon". Samson never realized that the contest was a battle between the God of Israel, whom he represented, and the god of the Philistines, the Dragon. ***The battle of Gods.***

> *Then the lords of the Philistines gathered them together for to offer a great sacrifice unto Dagon their god, and to rejoice: for they said, Our god hath delivered Samson our enemy into our hand. And when the people saw him, they praised their god: for they said, Our god hath delivered into our hands our enemy, and the destroyer of our country, which slew many of us. (Judges 16:23-24)*

Back to the story of my friend Kelvin. He got entangled with a lady he met in one of the hotels and began an unholy relationship with her. Apparently, the lady desperately wanted someone to marry, so she took Kelvin's name to her father who, by demonic means, turned Kelvin's heart away from his family and made him entirely devoted to the lady. Kelvin abandoned his wife and children and moved on with the lady.

Because he was no longer in his right mind, he began to underperform at work and eventually lost his job. He lost his relationships with the church, family and friends, and life became difficult for him. But unlike Samson, the church and Kelvin's wife continued to pray for him because it was apparent that he was under a demonic spell.

God delivered Kelvin and the spell on him got broken. He returned to his family and was reunited with the church.

Many men are not as lucky as my friend Kelvin because they lose everything, including their lives. Samson was also in this category. The lords of the Philistines were smart enough to damage Samson:

> *But the Philistines took him, and put out his eyes, and brought him down to Gaza, and bound him with fetters of brass; and he did grind in the prison house. (Judges 16:23)*

As Samson's hair began to grow back and his strength got restored, he cried to God and God answered him.

> *And Samson said, Let me die with the Philistines. And he bowed himself with all his might; and the house fell upon the lords, and upon all the people that were therein. So the dead which he slew at his death were more than they which he slew in his life. (Judges 16:30)*

These are not times when anyone should take things for granted. Engaging in adultery, fornication and the like will only expose a man to strange battles. A married man keeping extramarital affairs will be shocked if his eyes were opened to see the evil altars where the ladies he is immorally engaged with have taken his name and case to. Every lady on the street wants to protect and defend their sources of livelihood. The same also applies to married women engaged in extramarital affairs.

Your Involvement in this Battle

- You must be born again. This is not negotiable.
- You must live a holy life.
- You must know your God. Having a good relationship with God makes this possible.
- You must crucify the flesh.
- You must kill your inordinate affections and lust of flesh.
- You must avoid unholy friendships.
- You must associate more with the brethren who share common faith with you.
- You must be prayerful.

CHAPTER 3

King Nebuchadnezzar and the Three Hebrew Men

Thou shalt have no other gods before me. Thou shalt not make unto thee any graven image, or any likeness of any thing that is in heaven above,or that is in the earth beneath, or that is in the water under the earth. Thou shalt not bow down thyself to them, nor serve them: for I the Lord thy God am a jealous God, visiting the iniquity of the fathers upon the children unto the third and fourth generation of them that hate me

- Exodus 20:3-5

Shadrach, Meshach, and Abed-Nego answered and said to the king, "O Nebuchadnezzar, we have no need to answer you in this matter. If that is the case, our God whom we serve is able to deliver us from the burning fiery furnace, and He will deliver us from your hand, O king. But if not, let it be known to you, O king, that we do not serve your gods, nor will we worship the gold image which you have set up. (Daniel 3:16-18)

Some life situations will test our spiritual resolve. They may be issues raging against our health, marriage, career, finance, job, children, etc. Whatever they may be, God expects us to stand for him amidst any adversity.

Let your conversation be without covetousness; and be content with such things as ye have: for he hath said, I will never leave thee, nor forsake thee. (Heb. 13:5.)

There was a time at Babylon, when King Nebuchadnezzar was reigning. He was a powerful king, and his kingdom was well entrenched. In the third year of the reign of Jehoiakim king of Judah, King Nebuchadnezzar of Babylon came for Jerusalem and besieged it. He eventually captured it and took all the people into exile, in Babylon. God gave Jerusalem into his hand because of the atrocities of Jehoiakim, who was King of Judah at the time.

Shadrach, Meshach, and Abed-Nego were three Hebrew men in the kingdom of Babylon at the time. They were also Daniel's friends. Apparently, Daniel was not in the same province with them during their temptation. They were part of those taken by King Nebuchadnezzar from Judah.

Because of his arrogance and pride, King Nebuchadnezzar made a golden image and required everyone in the kingdom to bow to it. And whoever refused would be thrown into a furnace of fire which he already prepared.

Nebuchadnezzar the king made an image of gold, whose height was sixty cubits and its width six cubits. He set it up in the plain of Dura, in the province of Babylon. And King Nebuchadnezzar sent word to gather together the satraps, the administrators, the governors, the counsellors, the treasurers, the judges, the magistrates, and all the officials of the provinces, to come to the dedication of the image which King Nebuchadnezzar had set up. So the satraps, the administrators, the governors, the counsellors, the treasurers, the judges, the magistrates, and all the officials of the provinces gathered together for the dedication of the image that King Nebuchadnezzar had set up; and they stood before the image that Nebuchadnezzar had set up. Then a herald cried aloud: "To you it is commanded, O peoples, nations, and languages, that at the time you hear the sound of the horn, flute, harp, lyre, and psaltery, in symphony with all kinds of music, you shall fall down and worship the gold image that King Nebuchadnezzar has set up; and whoever does not fall down and worship shall be cast immediately into the midst of a burning fiery furnace. (Daniel 3:1-6)

Shadrach, Meshach, and Abed-Nego refused to bow to the image created by the King, choosing only to worship and serve the God of Israel. Their 'rebellious' act was reported to King Nebuchadnezzar who summoned the trio to appear before him. He rehearsed the instructions and expected Shadrach, Meshach, and Abed-Nego to bow down.

The King threatened, ***And who is*** the god who will deliver you from my hands? (Dan 3:15.)

The three Hebrew men refused to bow, and the king commanded that they be thrown into the furnace of fire.

Shadrach, Meshach, and Abed-Nego knew their God and His power to deliver from any situation. They made a most inspiring remark that even if God would not come to save them, they would rather die than to bow down to the god of the king. ***They knew it was the battle of Gods.***

The Story of Betty

Betty was a single Christian lady; everyone in the office knew her as such. She was the personal assistant to one of the General Managers of the company where she worked. She was well paid and enjoyed lots of benefits. Many ladies in the company envied her position.

Meanwhile, her boss kept pressurising her to sleep with him. She had successfully rebuffed the boss on many occasions with various tactics and excuses. However, one day, Betty fell into the trap of this boss. She committed a grave official mistake that guaranteed her dismissal. Her boss said to her: **"You either agree to my request or you are gone"**.

Betty was devastated and frightened. She allowed fear to prevail and forgot about her God and His power to deliver. She also made the mistake of confiding in a so-called friend, a Christian lady. Betty later discovered this same lady had been sleeping with other bosses in the company. Apparently, such a person was not capable of dishing out wholesome counsels.

> *Shadrach, Meshach, and Abed-Nego answered and said to the king, "O Nebuchadnezzar, we have no need to answer you in this matter. If that is the case, our God whom we serve is able to deliver us from the burning fiery furnace, and He will deliver us from your hand, O king. But if not, let it be known to you, O king, that we do not serve your gods, nor will we worship the gold image which you have set up. (Daniel 3: 16-18)*

King Nebuchadnezzar was furious and his countenance changed towards Shadrach, Meshach, and Abed-Nego. He commanded that the furnace be heated up seven times more than usual. He also commanded certain mighty men of valour, who *were* in his army, to bind them and cast them into the fiery furnace.

The Hebrew men were bound in their coats, trousers, turbans, and other garments, and were cast into the midst of the burning furnace. Everyone around went mute and watched keenly to see how these handsome men would be roasted. They greatly pitied the trio. Shadrach, Meshach, and Abed-Nego were however not bothered. They would rather die than deny God. They knew their God and resolved to do whatever it took to keep faith in Him.

The armed men, who bound Shadrach, Meshach, and Abed-Nego, were slain by the flame of the furnace—it was that intense. However, to the amusement of all, including the King, Shadrach, Meshach, and Abed-Nego stood upright amid the fire and a fourth man appeared therein with them.

> *Then King Nebuchadnezzar was astonished; and he rose in haste and* spoke, saying to his *counsellors, "Did we not cast three men bound into the midst of the fire?" They answered and said to the king, "True, O king." "Look!" he answered, "I see four men loose, walking in the midst of the fire; and they are not hurt, and the form of the fourth is like the Son of God. (Dan 3: 24-25)*

The king commanded the three Hebrew men to come out of the fire immediately. He acknowledged their loyalty to their God who had mightily saved them.

> *Nebuchadnezzar spoke, saying, "Blessed be the God of Shadrach, Meshach, and Abed-Nego, who sent His Angel and delivered His servants who trusted in Him, and they have frustrated the king's word, and yielded their bodies, that they should not serve nor worship any god except their own God! Therefore I make a decree that any people, nation, or language which speaks anything amiss against the God of Shadrach, Meshach, and Abed-Nego shall be cut in pieces, and their houses shall be made an ash heap; because there is no other God who can deliver like this. (Dan 3: 28-29)*

Betty gave in to her boss' request and the report of the incident was never released. Afterwards, Betty continued secretly with the unholy affair with the man. One Friday evening, when they thought everyone had left the office, the boss decided to sleep with Betty right in his office. While in the middle of the action, the Group HR Director, a no-nonsense man, came to see the GM in his office. And alas! He met both naked.

The following morning, the news of this show of shame was all over the company. Betty and her boss were summoned to a disciplinary committee and fired thereafter. Betty eventually lost the job for which she denied her God and compromised her faith.

And for Shadrach, Meshach, and Abed-Nego, the king promoted them for their loyalty to their God.

> ***Then the king promoted Shadrach, Meshach, and Abed-Nego in the province of Babylon. (Dan 3:30)***

Betty never recovered from the loss of her job and could not find another job for a very long time. But after some time, with prayers and several deliverance sessions, God had mercy on her and she got another job.

I guess Betty learnt her lesson the hard way.

Your Involvement in this Battle

- You must be born again. This is not negotiable.
- You must live a holy life.
- You must know your God. Having a good relationship with God makes this possible. Despite the intensity and fierceness of the burning furnace, Shadrach, Meshach, and Abed-Nego were not perturbed, neither did they deny God.
- You must know your enemies and their gods.
- Never succumb to the threats of the enemy.
- Trust God to the point of death.
- You must let the world know your stand when it comes to God. Don't sit on the fence. Don't compromise.
- Keep your eyes and focus on Jesus and not the problems or battles that confront you.
- Never deny your God, both in private and in public.

CHAPTER 4

Moses & King Pharaoh

"Let Go of What Doesn't Belong."

– Anonymous

> *And Pharaoh said, Who is the* Lord, *that I should obey his voice to let Israel go? I know not the* Lord, *neither will I let Israel go. And they said, The God of the Hebrews hath met with us: let us go, we pray thee, three days' journey into the desert, and sacrifice unto the* Lord our God; lest he fall upon us with pestilence, or with the sword. (Exodus 5:2-3)

Several years after the death of Joseph and the King Pharaoh who promoted him, things changed dramatically for the children of Israel who continued to grow in Egypt.

> *Now there arose up a new king over Egypt, which knew not Joseph. And he said unto his people, Behold, the people of the children of Israel are more and mightier than we: "Come on, let us deal wisely with them; lest they multiply, and it come to pass, that, when there falleth out any war, they join also unto our enemies, and fight against us, and so get them up out of the land." Therefore they did set over them taskmasters to afflict them with their burdens. And they built for Pharaoh treasure cities, Pithom and Raamses. (Exo. 1:8-11)*

Often, we may find ourselves in unpremeditated situations. In some of those times, it may be God testing our faith. Also, it could be because of battles the enemies wage to destroy us because of our faith in God.

For the latter, we may be fighting against some kind of gods and not realize it. We could even rationalize the situation and think perhaps the experience is not unique to us. The battle of gods is real!

The Case of Paul

I once had a dear friend called Paul, who was tied down with an incurable sickness. He spent lots of money and was already running bankrupt. He had visited renowned physicians and great hospitals to no avail. The pain got worse and looked terminal. He lost his job, and his career began to plummet. At one point, it became apparent that the sickness was a spiritual attack because it defiled all medical solutions.

He was a good young man full of life and heath before the attack. He went for several prayer sessions and deliverances but the condition persisted. Paul was a Christian brother who was fervent and resolute in his faith in God. He was introduced to some occultic places where he was promised healing. Just like the three Hebrew men, he said he would rather die than seek help from occultic places where they promised to heal him.

Meanwhile, he got to know that he was attacked spiritually by someone he offended unknowingly. So, the person tied down my friend Paul with sickness and would not let him go.

> *And they made their lives bitter with hard bondage, in morter, and in brick, and in all manner of service in the field: all their service, wherein they made them serve, was with rigour. (Exodus 1:14)*

The children of Israel cried to God in their bondage and God heard their cry.

> *And it came to pass in process of time that the king of Egypt died: and the children of Israel sighed by reason of the bondage, and they cried, and their cry came up unto God by reason of the bondage. And God heard their groaning, and God remembered his covenant with Abraham, with Isaac, and with Jacob. And God looked upon the children of Israel, and God had respect unto them. (Exodus 2:23-25*)

God raised Moses for the deliverance of the children of Israel. Right from his birth and when he eventually fled Egypt, it was apparent that he possessed the traits of a great deliverer. However, by leaving Egypt for Midian to work for his father-in-law, Jethro, Moses was drifting from God's plan. But when the time was ripe, God sent an Angel to summon Moses for the assignment.

> *And the angel of the LORD appeared unto him in a flame of fire out of the midst of a bush: and he looked, and, behold, the bush burned with fire, and the bush was not consumed. And Moses said, I will now turn aside, and see this great sight, why the bush is not burnt. And when the LORD saw that he turned aside to see, God called unto him out of the midst of the bush, and said, Moses, Moses. And he said, Here am I. (Exodus 3:2-4)*

God called Moses and appointed Aaron as a priest and a mouthpiece to support him. The message to Pharaoh, King of Egypt, was clear: ***"Let my people go".***

In life, many people are tied down by the forces of darkness that won't let them go. It gets worse when the afflicted person is unaware that he is in the midst of a battle of gods. Some would argue that they just happen to be in an unfortunate situation common to many others. Sometimes, in life, things are not as they appear.

> *And afterward Moses and Aaron went in, and told Pharaoh, Thus saith the LORD God of Israel, Let my people go, that they may hold a feast unto me in the wilderness. And Pharaoh said, Who is the LORD, that I should obey his voice to let Israel go? I know not the LORD, neither will I let Israel go. (Exodus 5:1-2)*

True to his words, King Pharaoh never allowed the Israelites to leave. And this is typical of all enemies. Once you are in their trap, they will never release you unless a higher power comes to deliver you.

My friend Paul continued to suffer for many days and years under the bondage of the wicked power. With the involvement of many powerful men of God, who were prayer warriors, it was confirmed that Paul's uncle was responsible for his mysterious sickness.

Paul's uncle was confronted, and people begged him to forgive and release Paul. When he discovered that his identity had been revealed, Paul's uncle confirmed he was responsible and would ensure that Paul died of the sickness because of what Paul's father did to him. Paul's father also died mysteriously at some point in the past.

When Paul realized the source of his predicament, he engaged more in prayers, together with the men of God.

King Pharaoh continued to torment the children of Israel. For some of the miracles done by Moses and Aaron to prove God's power, Pharaoh's magicians could replicate same. But at a point, the magicians bowed to the power of the God of Israel.

> *Then the magicians said unto Pharaoh, This is the finger of God: and Pharaoh's heart was hardened, and he hearkened not unto them; as the Lord* had said*. (Exodus 8:19)*

So, it was a ***battle of Gods***, and the magicians recognised that. As a Christian, we must not be ignorant of situations around us. We must always challenge the gods of our enemies with our God. We will always win every such battle.

Even after many miracles that caused pains to the Egyptians, King Pharaoh refused to budge. Thereafter, God told Moses and Aaron that He would give Pharaoh and his people the last kick and Pharaoh would let Israel go.

> *And the Lord said unto Moses, Yet will I bring one plague more upon Pharaoh, and upon Egypt; afterwards he will let you go hence: when he shall let you go, he shall surely thrust you out hence altogether. (Exodus 11:1)*

We must involve our God in our life battles. We must stop fighting alone and making the enemies mock us. We must learn to allow God to pass through the land of our enemies as He did in Egypt. The enemies cannot survive such an experience.

> *For I will pass through the land of Egypt this night, and will smite all the firstborn in the land of Egypt, both man and beast; and against all the gods of Egypt I will execute judgment: I am the Lord. (Exodus 12:12)*

And indeed, once there was an outcry throughout Egypt when all the first born were killed by the Angel of Destruction, King Pharaoh yielded and commanded Israel to leave his land immediately. The God of Israel prevailed against the gods of the Egyptians.

> *And it came to pass, that at midnight the LORD smote all the firstborn in the land of Egypt, from the firstborn of Pharaoh that sat on his throne unto the firstborn of the captive that was in the dungeon; and all the firstborn of cattle. And Pharaoh rose up in the night, he, and all his servants, and all the Egyptians; and there was a great cry in Egypt; for there was not a house where there was not one dead. And he called for Moses and Aaron by night, and said, Rise up, and get you forth from among my people, both ye and the children of Israel; and go, serve the LORD, as ye have said. Also take your flocks and your herds, as ye have said, and be gone; and bless me also. (Exodus 12:29-32)*

Paul's uncle also continued in his evil against Paul. And on a fateful night, he sent an arrow of darkness to Paul to finally end his life. Coincidentally, Paul and the pastors were having a prayer vigil. The arrow sent by Paul's uncle backfired and hit his first child, who was studying at one of the country's universities. The boy died immediately.

The news of the child's death was relayed to Paul's uncle in the morning, and he knew what went wrong. He went to his occultic power again and sent another arrow to kill Paul. This also backfired and hit him, making him blind. Miraculously, Paul's mysterious sickness disappeared. Eventually, Paul's uncle was stricken down with a stroke. And just like King Pharaoh, he begged Paul and the pastors to pray for him. The uncle died a few days after Paul became healed. The battle of Gods is real!

When hopes are dashed, opportunities crumble, disappointment stares at you, rejections and situations make you serve the people you are better than; when you are losing your rights and are being discriminated against, then know that Pharaoh's power is at work.

When faced with battles too hot for you, there are steps you must take. You must never take things for granted; otherwise, secretly, the enemies, through their gods, will continue to afflict you and eventually end your glorious life, even if you are a child of God.

Your Involvement in this Battle

- You must be born again. This is not negotiable.
- You must live a holy life.
- You must know your God. Having a good relationship with God will make this possible.
- You must crucify the flesh.
- You must be resolute, just like Job.
- You must never listen to the advice of people to seek other gods.
- You must realize it is a battle of Gods, and ensure you confront the enemy with your God, just like David.
- You must be prayerful. Fervency in prayers is key.
- However strong or wicked the enemy may seem, never forget that your God is stronger and mightier.

CHAPTER 5

Prophet Elijah & the Prophets of Baal

"In spiritual warfare, as a matter of necessity, when a higher power comes across a lower power, the lower power must bow."

-Dr DK Olukoya

> *Then Elijah said to the people, "I, even I only, am left a prophet of the* Lord, *but Baal's prophets are 450 men. Let two bulls be given to us, and let them choose one bull for themselves and cut it in pieces and lay it on the wood, but put no fire to it. And I will prepare the other bull and lay it on the wood and put no fire to it. And you call upon the name of your god, and I will call upon the name of the* Lord, *and the God who answers by fire, he is God." And all the people answered, "It is well spoken." (1 Kings 18:22-24)*

> *And in the thirty and eighth year of Asa king of Judah began Ahab the son of Omri to reign over Israel: and Ahab the son of Omri reigned over Israel in Samaria twenty and two years. And Ahab the son of Omri did evil in the sight of the* Lord above all that were before him. *And it came to pass, as if it had been a light thing for him to walk in the sins of Jeroboam the son of Nebat, that he took to wife Jezebel the daughter of Ethbaal king of the Zidonians, and went and served Baal, and worshipped him. And he reared up an altar for Baal in the house of Baal, which he had built in Samaria. And Ahab made a grove; and Ahab did more to provoke the* Lord God of Israel to anger than all the kings of Israel that were before him. (1 Kings 16:29-33)

Because of all the atrocities of King Ahab and his wife Queen Jezebel, God sent Prophet Elijah to declare His word against Samaria that there would be no rain for three and half years.

> *And Elijah the Tishbite, who was of the inhabitants of Gilead, said unto Ahab, As the* Lord God of Israel liveth, before whom I stand, there shall not be dew nor rain these years, but according to my word. (I Kings 17:1)

God honoured Prophet Elijah's word and there was no rain for three and half years.

Apostle Ayo Babalola

Dr Daniel Olukoya, the General Overseer of the Mountain of Fire and Miracles Ministry (MFM), told the story of Late Apostle Ayo Babalola, the founder of Christ Apostolic Church (CAC) in Nigeria in one of his messages. Sometime in the 1950s, Apostle Ayo Babalola was mightily used by God in south-western Nigeria. At that time, traditional worshippers and occultism were prevalent. The spread of Christianity was limited and occultic practices were pervasive. People were being subdued by the powers of occultic men and no one dared to challenge them.

The Apostle went to preach in one of the demonic towns and asked the king for a piece of land to build a church. The king, who was also an occultic person, gave the Apostle a piece of land in a forest called "forbidden". No one goes in there and comes out alive.

Apostle Babalola was delighted and thanked the king. He then took his prayer warriors and headed to the bush. They prayed and when they were about to start clearing the bush, Apostle Babalola prayed with a loud voice and said, "Oh God arise and let your enemies in this bush be scattered!"

Immediately, those with him started hearing movements like a crowd of people running, but no one saw anyone. It was apparent that some unseen forces in the bush were fleeing at the prayer of the man of God.

Like that time of Apostle Ayo Babalola, the people of Samaria also served Baal and neglected God. So, for three and half years, the city suffered drought. God ensured that Prophet Elijah was taken care of. He was fed by ravens and preserved by the widow of Zarephath.

> *So he arose and went to Zarephath. And when he came to the gate of the city, behold, the widow woman was there gathering of sticks: and he called to her, and said, Fetch me, I pray thee, a little water in a vessel, that I may drink. And as she was going to fetch it, he called to her, and said, Bring me, I pray thee, a morsel of bread in thine hand. And she said, As the LORD thy God liveth,*

> *I have not a cake, but an handful of meal in a barrel, and a little oil in a cruse: and, behold, I am gathering two sticks, that I may go in and dress it for me and my son, that we may eat it, and die. And Elijah said unto her, Fear not; go and do as thou hast said: but make me thereof a little cake first, and bring it unto me, and after make for thee and for thy son. (I kings 17: 10-13)*

At the expiration of the three and half years, God asked Prophet Elijah to appear before King Ahab. He challenged the king and his prophets of Baal to a contest on Mount Camel. This would be in the full glare of the children of Israel, who also supported the term of the contest as proposed by Prophet Elijah. Prophet Elijah concluded that ***in the battle of Gods*** that would follow, the god that answered by fire would be the true God the people should serve. This pleased everyone, including the prophets of Baal.

On the said date, on Mount Camel, the prophets of Baal, 450 of them, called on their god to bring down fire to consume the prepared sacrifice. Unfortunately, they got no answer. Prophet Elijah mocked them and asked them to shout louder, maybe their god had gone out to the market or was on a journey. They did so; still, there was no answer.

> *And it came to pass at noon, that Elijah mocked them, and said, Cry aloud: for he is a god; either he is talking, or he is pursuing, or he is in a journey, or peradventure he sleepeth, and must be awaked. And they cried aloud, and cut themselves after their manner with knives and lancets, till the blood gushed out upon them. And it came to pass, when midday was past, and they prophesied until the time of the offering of the evening sacrifice, that there was neither voice, nor any to answer, nor any that regarded. (I kings 18: 27-29)*

Once it was clear that Baal could not respond, Prophet Elijah stepped forward to take his part. He re-prepared the altar and asked that water be poured over it. He then called on the God of Israel, and straight away, fire came down from heaven and burnt up the sacrifice and the altar.

Then the fire of the LORD fell, and consumed the burnt sacrifice, and the wood, and the stones, and the dust, and licked up the water that was in the trench. And when all the people saw it, they fell on their faces: and they said, The LORD, he is the God; the LORD, he is the God. (I Kings 18: 38-39)

Also, in the case of Apostle Ayo Babalola, after his first prayer, there was calmness. Then a huge python appeared from the mountain opposite them and glided towards him. Those with him wanted to run away, but he ordered them to stay back and continue to cut the grass. The python continued to move towards him till it got very close. Apostle Ayo Babalola prayed again and said, "Let the fire of the God of Elijah fall on this python". Straight away, the python became stiff, as though it was electrocuted.

The news spread all over the town and nearby villages to the shock of the occultic men, including the king. That was the beginning of liberation for the people of the town. Many were also converted to Christ. The battle of Gods is real!

Your Involvement in this Battle

- You must be born again. This is not negotiable.
- You must live a holy life.
- You must know your God. Having a good relationship with God will make this possible.
- You must crucify the flesh.
- You must realize it is a battle of Gods, and ensure you challenge the enemy with your God.
- You must never be swayed by the number of the people against you. Only Prophet Elijah faced the 450 prophets of Baal.
- You must be prayerful and pray the kind of prayers that brings down fire from heaven.

CHAPTER 6

Gideon and the Midianites

"I can do all things through Christ who strengthens me."

– Philippians 4:13

> *So, Gideon built an altar to the LORD there and called it The LORD Is Peace. To this day it stands in Ophrah of the Abiezrites. That same night the LORD said to him, "Take the second bull from your father's herd, the one seven years old. Tear down your father's altar to Baal and cut down the Asherah pole beside it. Then build a proper kind of altar to the LORD your God on the top of this height. Using the wood of the Asherah pole that you cut down, offer the second bull as a burnt offering. (Judges 6:24-26)*

Sometimes, God may be preparing you so He could use you to chart a new course for your family, community or even country. Many times, people within a larger set could be crying to God secretly, seeking deliverance. And when God is ready to deliver them, He may need to raise up a Gideon for that purpose.

Once the Israelites turned their backs against God, He would always abandon them, and the enemies were quick to jump in. We saw such situation in Judges 6 when God left them to the mercy of the Midianites when they sinned against Him.

> *The Israelites did evil in the eyes of the LORD, and for seven years he gave them into the hands of the Midianites. Because the power of Midian was so oppressive, the Israelites prepared shelters for themselves in mountain clefts, caves and strongholds. (Judges 6:1-2)*

God never wants to leave any of His children, but when they step out of line, He is unable to defend them. The devil may have legal access to the life of such persons. The book of Isaiah 49:26 refers to ***"lawful captives".***

The Midianites plundered and impoverished the children of Israel for seven years. The Israelites lived in fear and intimidation. They were oppressed and wasted by the enemies, the Midianites.

Here is one good thing about God: Once a sinner retraces his step back to Him, He is always ready to receive and forgive him.

> *He that covereth his sins shall not prosper: But whoso confesseth and forsaketh them shall have mercy.* ***(Proverbs 28:13)***

The children of Israel cried to God because of their enemies, the Midianites, and God came to their rescue, sending them a deliverer.

> *Midian so impoverished the Israelites that they cried out to the LORD for help. When the Israelites cried out to the LORD because of Midian, he sent them a prophet, who said, "This is what the LORD, the God of Israel, says: I brought you up out of Egypt, out of the land of slavery. I rescued you from the hand of the Egyptians. And I delivered you from the hand of all your oppressors; I drove them out before you and gave you their land. I said to you, 'I am the LORD your God; do not worship the gods of the Amorites, in whose land you live.' But you have not listened to me. (Judges 6:6-10)*

God identified Gideon as the man for the assignment. The angel of the Lord appeared to him, and he was commissioned for the job. After accepting the task, he needed to deal with the issue of idolatry. He was instructed to clear out the idols of his father's house, which he did appropriately.

This is instructive. Whoever is ready for God's assignment must clear out all entanglements. Family idols, personal idols, etc. must be thrown out.

Adewale and the Family Idol

Adewale was a childhood friend; we were so close during our high school days. Back then, he was a very intelligent and active young boy. On several occasions, I went to his family house after school, especially when we engaged in joint studies, preparing for our promotional examinations.

We both gave our lives to Christ as teenagers and that also made us very close. However, one day, he told me one terrifying story about his family. His grandfather was an occultic man. He had a family idol and compelled all his children, including Adewale's father, to worship the idol. Whichever children that failed to worship the idol would develop a strange sickness and die.

All the man's children, seven of them, including Adewale's father, knew this and were scared to disobey their father's instruction. Annually, they would bring their respective children to the village for the celebration and worship of this family idol.

When Adewale became born again, he refused to go to the village to worship this family idol. He could do this because he had just gotten into the university and was away from home. His father instructed him to join them in the village for the annual ritual, which he refused. He told his father he had accepted Jesus. The grandfather discovered this and was furious with him.

The old man told Adewale's father that if the boy did not show up to take part in the annual worship and sacrifice to the family idol, he would die after seven days. Adewale's father was terrified and sad. He came with Adewale's mother to the university and begged Adewale. However, he refused and said he had accepted Jesus and could no longer worship any family idol with him.

So, Gideon chose men that would go to war with him against the Midianites once he got the assurance of God's presence with him.

> *Gideon and the hundred men with him reached the edge of the camp at the beginning of the middle watch, just after they had changed the guard. They blew their trumpets and broke the jars that were in their hands. The three companies blew the trumpets and smashed the jars. Grasping the torches in their left hands and holding in their right hands the trumpets they were to blow, they shouted, "A sword for the Lord* and for Gideon!" *While each man held his position around the camp, all the Midianites ran, crying out as they fled. (Judges 7:19-21)*

Once the children defeated the idols they once served, it was very easy for God to steps into their case. God is always ready to fight our battles if we don't have anything that can hinder Him. God stepped into the battle of the Midianites once the children of Israel, through Gideon, destroyed the altars of idols they kept. ***It's always the battle of Gods.***

Back to Adewale's story. He preached to his parents and assured them that the God he served would deliver him from whatever his grandfather and the family idol would do to him. Adewale's father became confident and also decided to give his life to Chris. He confronted his father and said they would no longer worship the family idol. The old man was incensed with indignation and went into his occultic room to invoke the power of the family idol to deal with Adewale and his father.

As he chanted several incantations and called Adewale's name and that of his father, something strange happened. What was intended to hit Adewale and his father backfired and hit the old man, Adewale's grandfather. The man fell and died on the spot.

That was how the whole family was liberated from the grip of a family idol. Hearing the news about what happened, the whole family turned to God and gave their lives to Christ.

It is good to know God and believe in His power to save. That knowledge will always draw people to God.

> *But the people that do know their God shall be strong, and do exploits. We all long to do great exploits. (Daniel 11:32)*

Your Involvement in this Battle

When faced with the battle against gods like a family idol, you should do the following:

- You must be born again. This is not negotiable.
- You must live a holy life.

- You must know your God. Having a good relationship with God makes this possible.
- You must crucify the flesh.
- You must realize it is a battle of Gods, and ensure you challenge the enemy with your God.
- You must never compromise. You may be ostracized by family, but you must stand for your God.
- You must avoid some family occasions or engagements, especially where a family idol is to be worshipped.
- You must be prayerful and pray the kind of prayers that brings down fire from heaven.
- Never trust your strength. Absolute reliance on God is the key.

CHAPTER 7

Prophet Jonah & the Storm

"You can run, run, run away from a lot of things in life, but you can't run away from yourself. And the key to happiness is to understand and accept who you are."

— Dale Archer

But the Lord hurled a great wind upon the sea, and there was a mighty tempest on the sea, so that the ship threatened to break up. 5 Then the mariners were afraid, and each cried out to his god. And they hurled the cargo that was in the ship into the sea to lighten it for them. But Jonah had gone down into the inner part of the ship and had lain down and was fast asleep. 6 So the captain came and said to him, "What do you mean, you sleeper? Arise, call out to your god! Perhaps the god will give a thought to us that we may not perish. (Jonah 1:4-6)

The Book of Jonah begins with an important assignment for Prophet Jonah. The Bible did not reveal prior life of the prophet, but one can conclude that for God to send anyone on an assignment, that person must be capable and responsible enough to deliver that message. God never wants anyone to perish, so He always wants a situation where everyone can come to repentance.

The Lord is not slow to fulfill his promise as some count slowness, but is patient toward you, not wishing that anyshould perish, but that all should reach repentance. (2 Peter 3:9)

Unlike most other persons that God has sent on various assignments, Jonah rejected God's call. Foolishly, he attempted to flee the presence of the Lord by taking a ship to foreign shores.

But Jonah rose up to flee unto Tarshish from the presence of the Lord, and went down to Joppa; and he found a ship going to Tarshish: so, he paid the fare thereof, and went down into it, to go with them unto Tarshish from the presence of the Lord. (Jonah 1:3)

One can rightly say that Prophet Jonah belongs to the category of people (Men of God) who likes their prophecy to come to pass. Jonah said he knew God could change His mind. Jonah is the kind of prophet who would be delighted that death visits you instantly once he prophesies that you will die because of your sins, even if you repent.

Hence, when God sent him to Nineveh to proclaim God's anger against the city because of their sins, he fled to Tarshish. God sent a storm that imperilled not only him but also his shipmates. It ruined the mariners' commercial prospects, as they were forced to throw all their cargo into the sea to lighten the ship (Jon. 1:5). Eventually, the storm threatened their very lives (Jon. 1:11).

The mariners perceived, from experience, that the storm was not ordinary. They felt like it might be the consequence of a god fighting against them. Apparently, their gods could not save them. When they realized that the problem was from the God of Prophet Jonah, they had to appease Him. ***It is the battle of Gods.***

> *Then the mariners were afraid, and cried every man unto his god, and cast forth the wares that were in the ship into the sea, to lighten it of them. But Jonah was gone down into the sides of the ship; and he lay, and was fast asleep. (Jonah 1:5)*

We should be discerning enough whenever we encounter an ugly situation to determine if it is not consequent to a battle involving some kind of gods. That way, we can invoke the power of the Almighty God to come to our defence.

When the mariners saw that others were calling on their gods but Jonah was sleeping, they challenged him and requested his identity. Jonah knew God and knew the storm was from Him, so he asked them to cast him into the sea. The sailors reluctantly accepted. When they tossed him off the ship, the storm abated and the danger to the mariners subsided (Jon. 1:12-15).

God calls a man so he can serve other people. Jonah's call was for the benefit of Nineveh. When he rejected God's guidance, not only did the people he was called to serve languish, those who surrounded him also suffered. If we accept that we are all called to serve God in our line of work, which is probably different from Jonah's work but no less important to God, then we would recognise that failing to serve God in our work is disadvantageous to our communities. The more powerful our gifts and talents, the greater the harm we can cause if we reject God's guidance in our work.

We can all recall people whose prodigious abilities enabled them to do great harm in different fields, be it business, government, society, science, religion, etc. Imagine the good they could have done or the evil they could have averted if they had submitted their skills first to the worship and service of the Lord. Our gifts may seem puny in comparison, yet imagine the good we can do and the evil we can avert if we do our work in service to God in our lifetime.

The Call of God on Pastor Adeola

Pastor Adeola was a vibrant man of God in Lagos, Nigeria, at a point in his ministry. He was a member of one of the fast-growing ministries in Lagos at that time, and signs and wonders happened through him. He was a great teacher of God's word too.

The ministry was going to spread its tentacles to some rural areas of the country and the names of some pastors to be transferred out of the state to these rural areas were submitted to the General Overseer of the ministry. After a period of seeking God's face in prayers, Pastor Adeola was one of those selected to be transferred.

That was when the problem started. He did not want to leave, and so he opposed the move. He claimed God did not tell him he would be transferred. The General Overseer of the ministry asked him to go to seek the Lord's face and report back to him. In anger, he never did.

When it was clear that he must be transferred to the remote community out of his so-called 'comfort zone', he opted to leave the church. He reckoned that God had been using him and it was time he started his own ministry.

Okene Village

Okene village was a remote community in Kogi State towards the northern part of Nigeria. Back in the day, the village was notorious for idol worshipping and terrible evil practices. People in the community were under serious bondage by occultic men who held everyone in the community captive.

The occultic practice of these men also required them to sacrifice humans to their gods at a particular period of the year. People were always warned not to come out at that time, especially from evening till dawn. Many who happened to be out during the curfew and entrapped were mostly strangers who were unfortunate to be in the community at that period and did not know the danger of flouting the warning of these occultic men.

Pastor Adeola had a son, his only child. He was, at the time, at the University of Ilorin. Ilorin is a city near Okene community. Though not within the same state, it shared boundaries with the community. People from both communities freely move across the cities and towns in both states.

Pastor Adeola's son, Michael, with a group of friends decided to visit Okene town on an educational tour. Unknown to them, it was during the period when these occultic men had warned everyone to stay indoor because of the idol worship and sacrifices they wanted to perform. Michael and his group of friends entered the community late that evening and were arrested by agents of these occultic men.

The king of the community was also a member of the occultic group, so there was no way of escape for these boys. To make matters worse, the Police department in the community were in the know and never interfered in the dealings of the community during that period. They always supported the evil men, maybe out of fear.

The occults would tie down their captives for three days and perform some rituals on them. Thereafter, they would sacrifice them to their gods.

Prophet Jonah was in the belly of the fish for three days and three nights. When he prayed to God in repentance, God made the fish to vomit him in Nineveh where He sent him in the first place.

> *But the LORD sent a great fish to swallow Jonah, and he remained in the belly of the fish three days and three nights. Jonah prayed to* ***the LORD, his God, from the belly of the fish: (Jonah 2:1-2)***

God answered Prophet Jonah after he prayed most possibly because God was really interested in the salvation of the entire nation of Nineveh.

> *Then the LORD commanded the fish to vomit Jonah upon dry land. (Jonah 2:11)*

Running away from God's assignment always portends danger not only for the people who are meant to be served but also to the messenger. God put His gift in you not for self-glory but for service to Him. He would surely determine where and when the gift should be used.

When Prophet Jonah proclaimed God's word and judgement on Nineveh, immediately, everyone, including the King, turned a new leaf. They repented, fasted and put on sack cloths as a sign of remorse.

> *When the news reached the king of Nineveh, he rose from his throne, laid aside his robe, covered himself with sackcloth, and sat in ashes. Then he had this proclaimed throughout Nineveh: "By decree of the king and his nobles, no man or beast, no cattle or sheep, shall taste anything; they shall not eat, nor shall they drink water. Man and beast alike must be covered with sackcloth and call loudly to God; they all must turn from their evil way and from the violence of their hands. Who knows? God may again repent and turn from his blazing wrath, so that we will not perish." When God saw by their actions how they turned from their evil way, he repented of the evil he had threatened to do to them; he did not carry it out. (Jonah 3:6-10)*

God would have expected Pastor Adeola to go to Okene community and use the gift He gave him to deliver the indigenes who were under occultic manipulation. Unfortunately, he did otherwise. He was devastated when he heard that his only son was captured. He and his wife prayed and fasted having realized their errors and the reason God had sent them to Okene in the first place.

Hurriedly, he travelled to Kogi State and then to Okene community. He also went with some prayer warriors, members of his team. When they arrived at Okene, it was already the third day and some of those captured by the occultic men had already been killed. Pastor Adeola and his men engaged the occults in a fierce battle. God fought for them and struck these men down. More than half of them died in the process and the few who remained surrendered to the power of Jesus. By the time Pastor Adeola would check the room where the captives were kept, alas! His only son and two other people had been killed by these men. Others were released.

Pastor Adeola and his wife wept uncontrollably because they knew that they caused the death of their only son. If they had listened to the voice and calling of God to come to the community early enough, they would have stopped the operations of the occultic men and saved many victims of their evil sacrifice.

The community was delivered and many turned to Christ. However, Pastor Adeola and his wife lived to regret their action. Immediately, they relocated to the community and continued the work of God.

Your Involvement in this Battle

- When there is a battle between God and other gods and God asks you to do some things, you must answer quickly.
- You must not entangle yourself with sin and worldliness.
- You must obey God to the letter.
- You must use whatever gift of God you possess wholly for God's assignment.

- You must realize it is a battle of Gods, and ensure you challenge the enemy with your God.
- You must never compromise. Never listen to contrary advice from people to persuade you to do otherwise.
- You must be prayerful. The devil and his men may want to turn the battle on you, so don't be complacent.
- If God chooses to change His mind, never complain. Just do as you are told. Prophet Jonah was not happy because God changed His mind and won't destroy the city of Nineveh after the people repented.

CHAPTER 8

Daniel in the Lion's Den

"Do not call conspiracy everything this people call a conspiracy; do not fear what they fear, and do not dread it."

- Isaiah 8:12

> *Then the king commanded, and Daniel was brought and cast into the den of lions. The king declared to Daniel, "May your God, whom you serve continually, deliver you!" And a stone was brought and laid on the mouth of the den, and the king sealed it with his own signet and with the signet of his lords, that nothing might be changed concerning Daniel. Then the king went to his palace and spent the night fasting; no diversions were brought to him, and sleep fled from him. Then, at break of day, the king arose and went in haste to the den of lions. As he came near to the den where Daniel was, he cried out in a tone of anguish. The king declared to Daniel, "O Daniel, servant of the living God, has your God, whom you serve continually, been able to deliver you from the lions?" Then Daniel said to the king, "O king, live forever! My God sent his angel and shut the lions' mouths, and they have not harmed me, because I was found blameless before him; and also before you, O king, I have done no harm. (Daniel 6: 16-22)*

Daniel also served during the reign of Darius, King of Babylon. He was dutiful and diligent because an excellent spirit was upon him. It pleased Darius to set over the kingdom one hundred and twenty satraps to be over the whole kingdom; and over these, three governors of whom Daniel *was* one, that the satraps might give account to them so that the king would suffer no loss.

Then Daniel distinguished himself from among the governors and satraps because an excellent spirit was in him. The king considered setting him over the whole realm. So, the governors and satraps sought to find some charge against Daniel concerning the kingdom but they could find no charge or fault because he was faithful, neither was there any error or fault found in him.

You know, everyone has a weakness. However, in Daniel's case, we cannot call his manner of life a weakness; it was a way to get him though. He would rather give away whatever would affect his relationship with God and hold on to his God.

The governors knew this aspect of him and decided to plot against him and his God. They made the King to sign a decree that no one should pray to any other god except the god of Babylon. Darius unwittingly signed the decree. And in those days, the decree of Medes and Persia once signed could not be altered.

> *So these governors and satraps thronged before the king, and said thus to him: "King Darius, live forever! All the governors of the kingdom, the administrators and satraps, the counsellors and advisors, have consulted together to establish a royal statute and to make a firm decree, that whoever petitions any god or man for thirty days, except you, O king, shall be cast into the den of lions. Now, O king, establish the decree and sign the writing, so that it cannot be changed, according to the law of the Medes and Persians, which does not alter." Therefore King Darius signed the written decree. (Daniel 6:6-9)*

Once they got the king to sign the decree, the governors set up a watch against Daniel. They knew perfectly that he would fall into their trap. Daniel saw the decree, went home, opened his windows and prayed to God, as usual. Unknown to him, he was being watched. The governors garnered enough evidence against him and they reported the case to the king.

It then dawned on King Darius that there was a conspiracy against Daniel. He really loved him, but he could not reverse the decree.

> *And the king, when he heard these words, was greatly displeased with himself, and set his heart on Daniel to deliver him; and he labored till the going down of the sun to deliver him. Then these men approached the king, and said to the king, "Know, O king, that it is the law of the Medes and Persians that no decree or statute which the king establishes may be changed." So, the king gave the command, and they brought Daniel and cast him into the den of lions. But the king spoke, saying to Daniel, "Your God, whom you serve continually, He will deliver you." Then a stone was brought and laid on the mouth of the den, and the king sealed*

it with his own signet ring and with the signets of his lords, that the purpose concerning Daniel might not be changed. (Daniel 6:14-17)

Peter's Experience at Welco Telecoms

Peter joined Welco Telecoms early in his career and the Managing Director of the Company liked him. He was diligent and hard-working. His work ethics were perfect and inspiring. Several times at the management meetings, the Managing Director would rebuke others who were average performers and compare them with Peter, who had just joined the company and was already performing efficiently.

Since joining the company, the revenue and other performance indicators had improved. At the end of his first year with Welco Telecoms, Peter was promoted to the delight of few who loved and appreciated him and to the envy of others who were jealous of his performance. After all, they had been at the company before him but the Managing Director never saw anything good in them.

In the second year and at his new role, Peter continued his stellar performance. Then the guys who never liked him conspired against him and sought to get him out of the company.

The Plot

Welco Telecoms was a reasonably big company. Most times, contracts were awarded to suppliers. The company took a tough stance against bribery and corruption. Meanwhile, prior to Peter's joining Welco Telecoms, those other guys oversaw contract awards to suppliers and always collected bribes before awarding those contracts.

When Peter joined the company, the Managing Director made him the head of the contract awarding committee. Hence, the unholy practice of bribery stopped. Those guys were never happy about this. When a new contract was to be awarded and bids were collected from registered suppliers, they connived with one of the suppliers to lower his bid, to win the bid.

In exchange for this favour, the supplier would send a huge amount to Peter's bank account. It would seem as though Peter demanded a bribe from him so that he could win the contract.

The plot worked as planned and those guys provided evidence of payment into Peter's account to the Managing Director. Peter was summoned and queried but he expressed his innocence. However, nobody believed him amongst the management team. The Managing Director was very sad because he loved him, but all the evidence available could not exonerate Peter. The company's policy must be followed. Peter was fired.

So, in the lion's den, Daniel continued his prayers to God, and God shut up the mouths of the lions and they could not hurt him.

Because of the love King Darius had for Daniel, he could not sleep all night and had to wait until the morning to see what had become of Daniel. Very early the following morning, the king rushed to the lions' den, opened it and called out Daniel.

> *Then the king arose very early in the morning and went in haste to the den of lions. And when he came to the den, he cried out with a lamenting voice to Daniel. The king spoke, saying to Daniel, "Daniel, servant of the living God, has your God, whom you serve continually, been able to deliver you from the lions? (Daniel 6:19-20)*

The king was delighted to know that Daniel's God saved him. He commanded that all the conspirators against Daniel be thrown into the lions' den instead.

> *And the king gave the command, and they brought those men who had accused Daniel, and they cast them into the den of lions—them, their children, and their wives; and the lions overpowered*

> *them, and broke all their bones in pieces before they ever came to the bottom of the den. (Daniel 6:24)*

King Dairus also honoured Daniel afterwards for all these troubles.

At Welco Telecoms, those guys were restored as head of contract awards, and they continued with their evil ways, steadily stealing from the company through those suppliers.

Not quite long afterward, one of the junior staff overheard them as they joked about how they plotted against Peter and got him sacked. He reported the case to the Managing Director. The Managing Director was enraged and queried them, but they all denied the allegation. He then reported the case to the Police. The Police investigator invited the supplier who transferred the cash to Peter's bank account. After thorough investigation and questionings, he confessed to the crime and the plot.

The Managing Director invited Peter back to the company and promoted him with other benefits. He was paid the backlog of salaries and entitlements from the date he was sacked. The Police charged those guys to court because they discovered they were also involved in several other frauds. They were eventually jailed.

Your Involvement in this Battle

If you ever find yourself in the battle of conspirators, ensure the following are true about you:

- You must be born again. This is not negotiable.
- You must live a holy life.
- You must know your God. Having a good relationship with God makes this possible.
- You must always maintain your principles. People will entice you to sway you from what you believe before their gods can fight you. Know that trick of the enemy.

- You must avoid unholy friendships.
- You must be prayerful. It will always do you good if your prayer life is always on fire.
- Let everyone know that you stand with God, both in private and in public.

CHAPTER 9

Sennacherib and King Hezekiah

There is a difference between conceit and confidence. Conceit is bragging about yourself Confidence means you believe you can get the job done.

- Johnny Unitas

The commander said to them, "Tell Hezekiah, 'Thus says the great king, the king of Assyria: On what do you base this trust of yours? Do you think mere words substitute for strategy and might in war? In whom, then, do you place your trust that you rebel against me? Do you trust in Egypt, that broken reed of a staff, which pierces the hand of anyone who leans on it? That is what Pharaoh, king of Egypt, is to all who trust in him. Or do you people say to me, "It is in the Lord our God we trust!"? Is it not he whose high places and altars Hezekiah has removed, commanding Judah and Jerusalem, "Worship before this altar in Jerusalem? (2 Kings 18:19-22)

King Hezekiah was one of the few kings in Judah who followed God wholeheartedly. From the beginning of his reign at the age of twenty-five, he delighted the Lord in all he did. He pulled down all the high places where the people worshipped other gods except God. He destroyed even the brazen serpent made by Moses, which the people had continued to make sacrifice to.

He never wanted to annoy the King of Assyria because he was the most powerful king at that time. Whatever he asked, King Hezekiah did to the extent of taking gold from God's temple to appease him.

Now in the fourteenth year of king Hezekiah did Sennacherib king of Assyria come up against all the fenced cities of Judah, and took them. And Hezekiah king of Judah sent to the king of Assyria to Lachish, saying, I have offended; return from me: that which thou puttest on me will I bear. And the king of Assyria appointed unto Hezekiah king of Judah three hundred talents of silver and thirty talents of gold. And Hezekiah gave him all the silver that was found in the house of the LORD, and in the treasures of the king's house. (2 Kings 18:13-15)

However, King Sennacherib of Assyria was never content. He wanted the people of Judah to be completely subdued and serve him. Also, he disdained the God of Judah and compared Him with other gods. He told the people of Judah not to believe that God would save them seeing that the gods of other people could not deliver them from his hands.

> *Do not listen to Hezekiah, for thus says the king of Assyria: Make peace with me, and surrender to me! Eat, each of you, from your vine, each from your own fig tree. Drink water, each from your own well, until I arrive and take you to a land like your own, a land of grain and wine, a land of bread and vineyards, a land of rich olives and honey. Live, and do not die! And do not listen to Hezekiah when he would incite you by saying, 'The LORD will rescue us.' Has any of the gods of the nations ever rescued his land from the power of the king of Assyria? Where are the gods of Hamath and Arpad? Where are the gods of Sepharvaim, Hena, and Ivvah? Did they indeed rescue Samaria from my power? Which of the gods for all these lands ever rescued his land from my power? Will the LORD then rescue Jerusalem from my power? (2 Kings 18:31-35)*

As in the case of King Hezekiah, sometimes in life, ugly situations or enemies will try to frustrate you, make disparaging comments about your God, and even question the power of your God to deliver you. They will be so arrogant because they have dealt with other people and crushed them even though those people relied on their gods for deliverance. They make a mistake by thinking the Almighty God is as powerless as those gods they have conquered. They are always boastful and insulting, always so confident in their gods and magic because they had gotten results on several occasions.

Egbeda Community

The security situation was so horrible at Egbeda community back in the 80s. Egbeda community is in Lagos state, south-west Nigeria. During that period, the community was seriously terrorized by a group of armed robbers. The robbers were powerful, not only because they were armed but also because they had "voodoo" power. Their leader was a very powerful occultic man. The robbers were feared by all, including the local Police. Even the National Police Authority dreaded them because they were politically connected. No one dared to challenge them.

They terrorized all the communities in Egbeda for a very long time until a young believer moved to one of the apartments in the community. His name was Brother James. He was a believer and a very prayerful Christian.

When Brother James moved into an apartment in one of the streets in the community, some of his neighbours queried why he chose to come to that area without enquiring about its security situation. They told him about all that had bedevilled them and how they were being terrorized by the armed robbers. Brother James was unfazed by this news because he knew his God. Meanwhile, the terrors always knew when new folks move into the area, so they knew when Brother James came into the community.

On a particular occasion, the armed robbers wrote to the community heads and demanded that money be contributed to appease them. The communities involved gladly did that, yet the robbers would not let them be. Brother James, now aware of the nefarious activities of these criminals, engaged the Lord in serious prayer and fasting. Some of his neighbours also joined him, and every night, they gathered for a vigil. Gradually, the people who had lived in fear before began to gain confidence in God and refused to give tribute to these armed robbers.

The robbers became furious and wrote the communities that they would strike at a particular night and whosoever does not keep cash for them would be killed. When the community head got this letter, he called Brother James and some of the brethren. Brother James and every other willing heart declared another fasting and continued their vigils.

A day prior to when the armed robbers would strike, they were all together and drank alcohol heavily. There was no power supply, so they put on the generator. After a while, they all fell asleep while the generator continued to work.

Unfortunately, the smoke from the generator, which was close to the window, filtered into the apartment where the robbers slept and choked them all in their sleep, and they all died.

It was a shout of joy in the morning when the news went around the communities that the robbers had died in their sleep. The people called the local Police, and their bodies were deposited at the morgue.

The community head, all the chiefs, and Brother James and the brethren gave special thanksgiving to the Lord for the great deliverance. Even the local Police confirmed that only God could have made their deaths possible. Everyone knew how powerful the charms and magical powers of the gang leader was. However, when God decided to come into the battle, both the charms and their gods could not save them. The children of God and the entire community were set free. Even the local Police, who had been under some kind of fear, were relieved.

After receiving the bad news and the insult from the servant of King Sennacherib, King Hezekiah rent his clothes, covered himself with sackcloth, and went into the house of the Lord. He also sent words to the Prophet Isaiah to inquire from God.

> *So, the servants of king Hezekiah came to Isaiah. And Isaiah said unto them, Thus shall ye say to your master, Thus saith the Lord, Be not afraid of the words which thou hast heard, with which the servants of the king of Assyria have blasphemed me. Behold, I will send a blast upon him, and he shall hear a rumour, and shall return to his own land; and I will cause him to fall by the sword in his own land. (2 Kings 19:5-7)*
>
> *And Hezekiah prayed before the Lord, and said, O Lord* God of Israel, which dwellest between the cherubims, thou art the God, even thou alone, of all the kingdoms of the earth; thou hast made heaven and earth. *Lord, bow down thine ear, and hear: open, Lord, thine eyes, and see: and hear the words of Sennacherib, which hath sent him to reproach the living God. Of a truth, Lord, the kings of Assyria have destroyed the nations and*

their lands, And have cast their gods into the fire: for they were no gods, but the work of men's hands, wood and stone: therefore they have destroyed them. Now therefore, O LORD our God, I beseech thee, save thou us out of his hand, that all the kingdoms of the earth may know that thou art the LORD God, even thou only. (2 Kings 19:15-19)

With much prayers, God sent Prophet Isaiah to tell King Hezekiah that he had heard him.

Then Isaiah the son of Amoz sent to Hezekiah, saying, Thus saith the LORD God of Israel, That which thou hast prayed to me against Sennacherib king of Assyria I have heard. (2 Kings 19:20)

God also assured the King that he would defend and protect the city.

Therefore thus saith the LORD concerning the king of Assyria, He shall not come into this city, nor shoot an arrow there, nor come before it with shield, nor cast a bank against it. By the way that he came, by the same shall he return, and shall not come into this city, saith the LORD. For I will defend this city, to save it, for mine own sake, and for my servant David's sake. (2 Kings 19: 32-34)

That night, the angel of the LORD went out and smote in the camp of the Assyrians One Hundred and Eighty-five thousand soldiers of King Sennacherib. And when they arose early in the morning, behold, they were all dead corpses.

When Sennacherib king of Assyria realized that virtually all his soldiers were dead, he departed to Nineveh. And his two sons killed him there.

And it came to pass, as he was worshipping in the house of Nisroch his god, that Adrammelech and Sharezer his sons smote him with the sword: and they escaped into the land of Armenia. And Esarhaddon his son reigned in his stead. (2 Kings 19: 37)

The God of Israel and King Hezekiah prevailed over the god of King Sennacherib the Assyrian. ***It was the battle of Gods.***

Your Involvement in this Battle

If you ever find yourself in a battle or the siege of the enemy where the enemy is boasting that your God cannot deliver you from his hand, the following should be your part:

- You must be born again. This is not negotiable.
- You must live a holy life.
- You must know your God. Having a good relationship with God makes this possible.
- You must never be afraid whatsoever the enemy may do.
- You must surrender the battle to God. Let God do the fighting.
- You can go into intense prayer and fasting.
- Never be scared because of the enemy's boastful and threatening words. Your God is stronger and mightier; always remember that.

CHAPTER 10

Your Prayer Altar

Satan is too serious to fight individuals.
He fights dreams, he fights prophetic programmes,
he fights mantles

- Apostle Joshua Selman.

Peter therefore was kept in prison: but prayer was made without ceasing of the church unto God for him. (Acts 10:5)

If God opens your eyes to see the battles going on as you pray, you will never stop again and never will you be depressed if your answers are delayed.

The common weapon for all forms of battles of Gods is prayer. You cannot be at war and be a lazy Christian. The stronger your prayer life, the quicker you will dismantle the strongholds of darkness. Daniel was a man of prayer as we saw earlier; he knew his God. There was a time he had to pray and the prince of Persia hindered his answers. His persistence in prayers caught God's attention, who had earlier approved his request. After due investigation, God dispatched a powerful angel, Michael, to clear the way and grant answers to Daniel's prayers.

Then said he unto me, Fear not, Daniel: for from the first day that thou didst set thine heart to understand, and to chasten thyself before thy God, thy words were heard, and I am come for thy words. But the prince of the kingdom of Persia withstood me one and twenty days: but, lo, Michael, one of the chief princes, came to help me; and I remained there with the kings of Persia. (Daniel 10:12-13)

When you become weak at the altar of prayers, you also weaken the angels fighting on your behalf. Your prayers energise the angels to continue in the battle.

Many things can also contribute to the weakening of your prayer altar. Some of them are:

- Sin — Psalm 66:18
- Unholy friends, bad associations — 1 Corinthians 5:11
- Laziness — Proverbs 13:4
- Forsaking the assembly of the saints — Hebrews 10:25

- Worldliness 1 John 2:15-17
- Corrupt communication Ephesians. 4: 29-32
- Lust 1 Corinthians 6:18-20
- Unforgiveness Matthew 6:15

We often hear this common line: ***"A prayerless Christian is a powerless Christian."*** This saying is true in all its ramifications. Life is a battlefield, and as a Christian, you cannot afford not to be a person of prayer. The Apostle Paul admonished us in 1 Thessalonians 5:17 to "Pray without ceasing".

We are all on the battlefield of life; whether we believe it or not is irrelevant. Meanwhile, there is no middle ground. It's either you fight and win or you are defeated and killed.

How do You Keep Your Spiritual Fire Burning?

The scriptures advise us to always keep the fire on our prayer altar burning. ***"The fire shall ever be burning upon the altar; it shall never go out." (Leviticus 6:13)***

The following are the answers to this question:

1. **Godly Repentance:** The scriptures say "he that keeps his sin will not prosper but whoever confesses and forsakes them shall have mercy" Proverbs 28:13. So, we must ensure to confess and forsake all known and unknown sins. Do well to run far away from sin and its appearances. And where you fall into any sin, God requires immediate repentance. David said, **"A broken and contrite heart you, God, will not** despise" (Psalms 51: 17).
2. **Baptism of the Holy Spirit:** The baptism of the Holy Spirit can also strengthen your prayer life, with the evidence of speaking in tongues. Speaking and praying in the Holy Spirit helps your

prayer altar and confuses the devil. It also empowers you to war in the spirit.

> But ye shall receive power, after that the Holy Ghost is come upon you: and ye shall be witnesses unto me both in Jerusalem, and in all Judaea, and in Samaria, and unto the uttermost part of the earth. (Acts 1:8.)

3. **Daily Prayers:** To keep the fire on your altar burning, a daily prayer life is inevitable. It's like the fuel to a burning fire. It therefore must be applied daily and more frequently. Prayer is equally the food of the Spirit. Hence, **"Pray without ceasing" (1 Thessalonians** 5:17).

4. **Daily Bible Study:** More importantly is the daily study of the scriptures. God told Joshua that to be successful, the book of the law should not depart from his mouth.

> This book of the law shall not depart out of thy mouth; but thou shalt meditate therein day and night, that thou mayest observe to do according to all that is written therein: for then thou shalt make thy way prosperous, and then thou shalt have good success. (Joshua 1:8)

Daily bible reading and studying ensures your prayers would be guided by the Holy Spirit. How much of God's word you know will help to align your prayers in the right direction and ensure a quick reaction from the throne of grace.

5. **Fasting & Meditation:** Maintaining the fire on your altar also requires you to fast and meditate frequently. A prayer session, coupled with fasting, is a potent spiritual weapon. Jesus also mentioned in Matthew 17:21 that some situations can only be resolved when prayer is backed by fasting.

6. **Evangelism and Sharing Your Testimonies:** To ensure that the fire on your prayer altar keeps burning, you must always engage

in evangelism. Jesus commanded everyone to go into the world and preach the good news He has given us.

> And he said unto them, Go ye into all the world, and preach the gospel to every creature. (Mark 16:15)

When you thoroughly obey this instruction, there will never be a hindrance to your prayers.

7. **Growing in the Production of the Fruits of the Holy Spirit:** Galatians 5:25 says "If we live in the Spirit, let us also walk in the Spirit". Meanwhile, Galatians 5:22-24 highlighted some elements of the fruit of the Spirit expected to be evident in our lives: **love, joy, peace, long-suffering, gentleness, goodness, faith, meekness,** and **temperance.**

8. **Forgiveness:** Another important thing that can help your prayer altar and keep the fire burning is your ability to forgive others who hurt you. Being forgiving ensures prayers are unhindered. Jesus clearly gave an admonition to this end with the attendant danger unforgiveness can have on our prayers to God.

> For if ye forgive men their trespasses, your heavenly Father will also forgive you: But if ye forgive not men their trespasses, neither will your Father forgive your trespasses. (Matthew 6:14-15).

CHAPTER 11

Rules of Spiritual Warfare

War has rules,

mud wrestling has rules,

politics has no rules.

- Ross Perot

1. Know your God: Dan. 11:32 ***"...but the people that do know their God shall be strong and do exploits"***. Know that God is your strength in the battle.

2. Know yourself: You must know your limitations, weaknesses and strengths. If your mouth, eyes, body, ears, etc. are your problem, know how to deal with them quickly.

3. Know your enemy: Find a way to probe the enemy. Discover the secret of the enemy, his hidden intentions. See 2 Corinthians 2:11.

4. Do not depend on human resources but only on heavenly resources: God's resources are more potent. See 2 Corinthians 10:4-5.

5. Fear God more than the enemy.

6. Employ highly accurate spiritual weapons. One weapon may work and the other may not. Employ the best and most effective one for each unique battle.

7. Exploit the enemy's weakness: Strike at the enemy's weakness. ***"Every Goliath has an unprotected forehead."*** *Dr DK Olukoya*

8. Learn to fight and learn to flee. Learn to retreat and re-fire. That way, you will have time to plan for a counter-move.

9. Learn to cut off the enemy's supply system: For every enemy, there is a power base. Learn how to cut off the power base of that enemy.

10. Any sin in your life will strengthen the enemy: Whenever sin is present, heaven moves away, and this opens the door for the enemy.

11. Take time to examine prevailing situations thoroughly before waging war. Don't go into the war casually. Be strategic.

12. Discover your advantages and use them.

13. Analyse the strength and weaknesses of the enemy and use them.

14. Know your weapons: Know all your spiritual weapons:

    - The Blood of Jesus
    - The Fire of the Holy Ghost
    - The Word of God
    - The Sword of the Spirit
    - Whirlwind
    - East Wind, etc.

    A single weapon may not bring the enemy down. It might require combinations of many weapons. That's why David took five stones, not just a stone.

15. Your enemy will always take advantage of your distress. Every panic, every distress of a believer is an advantage to the enemy.

16. Learn to identify the strategies of the enemy and scatter them.

17. Perform surprise attacks: If the enemy knows your pattern of prayers and Bible reading, such pattern may become ineffective.

    Don't be stereotyped. Do spiritual activities outside your normal routine. Pray at unexpected times and places. It can take the enemy unaware and hit them hard. Just as in a physical warfare, one of the potent ways of attack is a surprise attack.

18. Small rarely defeats large: When your strength is small, you will most likely be defeated.

19. Knowing how to win does not mean you will win. You must apply your knowledge correctly.

20. In spiritual warfare, victory goes to the hardest and meanest. The scripture compares spiritual warfare to a wrestling match where

there is no or little rules i.e. "we wrestle…" unlike a boxing match that is guided by rules.

21. Know that defensive tactics are different from offensive tactics.

22. Keep your enemy confused about the route of your attack.

23. Seek adequate spiritual knowledge. Don't go into spiritual battles without adequate knowledge. See Hosea 4:6.

24. Do not abandon the enemy's initiative. Take the initiative first. It shows you are brave. It also confuses the enemy. David ran towards Goliath. His action confused Goliath who was used to people running away from him.

25. Starve your enemy. Apart from sin, your doubt or faithlessness can feed the enemy.

26. Let your enemy find you unpredictable. Be mysterious.

27. Utilise the hours of the night in your warfare.

28. Ensure that the prince of this world has nothing on you, just like he did not have on our Lord Jesus Christ. See John 4:30.

29. Learn how to quickly adapt to changes in circumstances. Don't be caught off-guard.

30. Vary your tactics when necessary.

31. Worry will lead to blunders and strengthen the enemy.

32. You must be disciplined.

33. You must know your battlefield; otherwise, the enemy will mess you up.

References

You are in the boxing ring of life,

you either fight or you perish

– Dr. DK Olukoya

1. The picture of David & Goliath: David and Goliath retold…. When does the underdog win? | by Mark J Attard | Medium

2. The picture of Samson & Delilah: Was Samson's true weakness his hair or Delilah? (nationalgeographic.com)

3. The picture of King Nebuchadnezzar: imgurl:https://steemitimages.com/1280x0/https://cdn.steemitimages.com/DQmVda1jKVeKeUy-EuCfpjzXjUuFd7GMhGUZzZF98q3xpuvR/unnamed.jpg - Search (bing.com)

4. The picture of Moses & King Pharaoh: Were the miracles done by Moses considered to be magic by the subjects of the pharaohs? - Quora

5. The picture of Prophet Elijah & the Prophet of Baal: Old Testament 4, Lesson 4: Elijah and the Prophets of Baal - Seeds of Faith Podcast (cph.org)

6. The picture of Gideon & The Medianites: https://www.pinterest.com/pin/518406607078944283/

7. The picture of Prophet Jonah & the Storm: The Runaway Prophet & The Storm Calmer: injarsofclay — LiveJournal

8. Jonah's Call and Response (Jonah 1:1-17) | Theology of Work https://www.theologyofwork.org/old-testament/the-twelve-prophets/jonah-and-gods-blessing-for-all-nations/jonahs-call-and-response-jonah-11-17/

9. The picture of Daniel in the Lions' Den: https://www.gettyimages.com/detail/news-photo/peter-paul-rubens-flemish-painter-defeat-of-sennacherib-news-photo/517647603

10. The picture of the defeat of Sennacherib soldiers https://www.gettyimages.com/detail/news-photo/peter-paul-rubens-flemish-painter-defeat-of-sennacherib-news-photo/517647603

11. Angel Praying Images https://stock.adobe.com/search?k=angel+praying&asset_id=557045804

12. https://www.istockphoto.com/vector/death-king-gm519252817-49427304

13. 70 Rules of Spiritual warfare 70 RULES OF SPIRITUAL WAR-FARE WITH DR. D.K. OLUKOYA (youtube.com)

14. Bible References- King James Bible Version

www.ingramcontent.com/pod-product-compliance
Lightning Source LLC
LaVergne TN
LVHW091028150826
845672LV00006BA/1739

* 9 7 8 9 7 8 6 0 6 9 2 9 6 *